Front Cover Design:

Painting titled. "Subtle Seduction"

By Artist, Lidia Wylangowska

DEAR WIVES,

YOUR HUSBANDS WANT A GIRLFRIEND TOO

by *Donna Bunch Coaxum*

Speakinfaith Press

This book is dedicated to

the memory of my grandmother,

Nevador Shepherd;

my mother, Freddie Mae Bunch;

and my mother-in-law, Myrtle Coaxum.

CONTENTS

PREFACE ix

Chapter One

The Tipping Point 1

Chapter Two

Why? 13

Chapter Three

Communication: Two Parts Listening;
One Part Speaking 19

Chapter Four

Can You Handle The Truth? 31

Chapter Five

You Have Power 49

Chapter Six

Do The Right Thing 59

Chapter Seven

The Whole Truth 63

Chapter Eight

Would You Marry You? 77

ACKNOWLEDGEMENTS 81

PREFACE

My secret was out. A girlfriend of mine, in a routine visit to my closet — this time to see a killer pair of boots I had found on sale — happened to notice a flirty mini-skirt suit hanging there. She practically blew a gasket, and screamed, "What is this?!"

I casually responded, in a "matter-of-fact, checking-my-manicure" sort of way, "That's, one of my 'girlfriend' outfits." Her eyes rolled upward and, with that tell-tale crease furrowing her forehead, she posed her question simply, concisely, and incredulously, "WHAT?"

I could appreciate that her surprise appeared to be centered on the fact that I, a somewhat conservative, now nearly 20 year married mother and attorney would wear such an outfit at this point in my life. When I sat her down to explain my little secret to preserving the vitality of my marriage, my friend appreciated hearing that this outfit was one that my husband had actually purchased for me. Now, she was getting a different perspective on things. The wearing of the girlfriend outfits along with other behaviors and practices that I consciously chose to exhibit in my marriage comes out of what has been absolutely confirmed for me — my husband's desire to hold on to the "me" he'd fallen in love with. Like a lot of the husbands that I polled and interviewed for this book, my husband continues to crave some of the "girlfriend" in me that he enjoyed so much during our courtship.

I went on to tell my girlfriend that I had several of these "girlfriend" outfits, even pulled some down from my closet to give her a full visual. More importantly, I explained that I had stumbled upon some valuable information which I was sure would be helpful to all of us wives who hope to keep vitality and sparkle in our marital relationships.

Let me tell you where this whole thing began: One day I overheard my husband negatively describe another man's wife as "looking like a wife," and after receiving feedback from my husband, as well as from other husbands and ex-husbands, I have come to some conclusions about my interpretation of my husband's scathing "looking like a wife" comment. It seemed that such a statement meant that being and looking like a wife was the diametric opposite of looking and acting like a girlfriend. I wondered if the two could successfully coexist in one body. Could a wife be a girlfriend, too?

After I received a few responses from other husbands and ex-husbands, which seemed to confirm my suspicions about how husbands felt, I expanded and enlarged my inquiry to ensure that the information I had initially received was not based on an anomaly.

I decided to test this "girlfriend hypothesis." I thought back to my own days as a girlfriend; I considered what it was about that time that I believed had inspired my husband to ask me to be his wife. What was the watershed? After taking some time to truly reflect, I realized that during that time as a girlfriend on the brink of marriage, I had been *emotionally, financially, physically, professionally* and *spiritually* where I wanted to be in life. I was comfortable, independent, or, at the very least, confidently well on my way to achieving these five prongs. If I had to sum it up in two words, I would simply say that I considered myself to be "market ready."

Let's liken it to grocery shopping: Usually, consumer products companies don't like to put products on the market for sale unless they are market ready, including considerations of content, quality, placement, and packaging. As a "girlfriend," I was market ready. Being market ready gave me the confidence to be comfortable with my independence, and equally comfortable with the prospect of interdependence. As a result, I had no issues with my then boyfriend wanting to feel as if he were the "king of everything" when he was with me.

As I evaluated my role as wife several years later, I realized that at some point in my marriage I had lost some of the "girlfriend" in me. A couple of the five prongs had gone missing and I was no longer "market ready." After the conversation with my husband, however, I decided to revive the girlfriend in me. Hence, I got to work on becoming market ready all over again.

The great thing about revving up the "girlfriend" in me is that I did not have to work on all five of the prongs that I determined a fully accomplished girlfriend to have acquired. I had a few of these areas already in excellent operational mode. I put my plan into action, and, "Bingo!" I struck gold! This renewed "girlfriend" model created fireworks! My husband and I went into a honeymoon phase all over again. Now what do I do with this newly discovered information? I could not, in good conscience, keep it to myself.

I set out on a mission to inform and encourage ALL wives to continue stoking the fire that led them to the marriage altar or to relight it, if the embers had gone cold—to revive the girlfriend inside of them. Every lady remembers that hot number she was when she snagged that husband. I also set out to reach those still-single sisters who have a desire to get married, to ignite the "girlfriend factor" and keep it burning. I wanted to let them know that you don't let that factor go by the wayside after you say "I do." In essence: get, be, and stay "market ready."

While some readers, because of my "market ready" concept, may get the misconception that I am encouraging wives to set themselves up in a position to leave their husbands, that is absolutely not my thrust at all. What I am telling wives is that when you are "market ready" you're creating a "win-win" situation for you and for your husband. He gets to keep the girlfriend he was originally drawn to, while you get to hold on to the security of a vivacious, and hopefully, enduring marriage. Wives that maintain their "market readiness" keep alive that girlfriend that their husbands continue to desire.

Now, don't get me wrong; I'm talking about a "can't lose" proposition here, pretty much risk-free for everyone concerned. If a situation arises where the husband decides that he doesn't want to uphold his commitment to the marriage, or, for some other reason, the marriage dissolves, then here's a wife who won't have to drown herself in a laundry list of things that she needs to do in order to get back on the market. A woman who keeps herself on top of her game will already be emotionally, financially, physically, professionally and spiritually where she needs to be (or well on her way) in order to get back on "the market," if that is her desire. Now, you see, there is a dual advantage to being simultaneously a wife and girlfriend! Both wife and husband win. We're about to focus on being that woman who is a winner in the marital AND in the singles arena. So let's get our WaG (Wife and Girlfriend) on, ladies! Are you ready to truly be a M.R.S. ... A "Market Ready Sister" or, better yet, a "Market Ready Soul mate"? Then read on.

CHAPTER ONE

The Tipping Point

"I've always believed that you can think positive just as well as you can think negative." - James Baldwin

It was a beautiful weekend in March, and my husband, along with a group of his friends, had just returned from attending an athletic tournament in North Carolina. The event featured men's and women's basketball competitions. It was a huge occasion, attended by over 175,000 fans.

As with any sporting event, whose young players have the potential to enter the professional ranks, this tournament had its share of real sports fans, celebrities, and groupies. Besides the basketball competition, many folks converged on Charlotte, NC, for the concerts, after-parties, and simply to see and to be seen — to enjoy great socializing. Because this was my husband's first time attending the tournament, I was very interested in what he had experienced. I had a million questions, but never got beyond the first two.

The first answer was as simple as the question. Did he have fun? "Yes." It was his response to the next question that rocked my brain, and set me on this path of discovery. That answer gave me details beyond the simple "yes" answer he gave to my first question. There was as much to learn from what he didn't say as from what little he said. I asked him to tell me about the weekend, to fill me in on the details of what he did during his brief boys' getaway. He appeared to be as excited as a young man lost in the luxurious adventure of buying his first car.

He lit up and replied exuberantly, "It was great!" I could not let the conversation end there, especially considering how much excitement was in his voice and facial expression. The pregnant pause after the word "great" kept me wanting more, and wondering what made him describe the event so enthusiastically. I noticed that he passed on other, more general descriptors, like "good," "enjoyable," and "fun." He was really excited about the experience, and I had to know more.

When he described the basketball matches he attended, he seemed so much more energized about it than the usual good time. As he named the celebrities and high profile folks who attended, he spoke of the many guys who showed up driving their Bentleys and Rolls Royces, and how stylish they all were.

He went on to describe a particular businessman who attended, and then the excitement in his voice came to a screeching halt. He paused, his eyes rolled, and said, "Oh, yeah, then there was so-and-so's [the businessman's] wife, looking like a wife."

I gasped at that description! This particular businessman, (who shall remain nameless) is a multi-millionaire, who really does look like the money he purportedly earns each year. His wife, who has been with him for quite a while, seemingly gets no attention for the part she has played in their success. Nevertheless, the deflation in my husband's voice snatched my attention and put me somewhat on the defensive, I must admit. I wanted him to keep talking, so, in order to keep him from shutting our conversation down, I took a breath, and calmly asked him what he meant by the phrase "looking like a wife." I was also asking myself some questions. "When did the word 'wife' become an adjective? Did other husbands talk like this when hanging with their married guy-friends? And what did my husband say about me in those circles?"

I digress. My husband slowly swallowed the bit of food he was chewing, and casually responded as if I had asked some innocuous question whose answer was a no-brainer. He said, "You know what I mean, looking all dumpy and dowdy." He never missed a beat in his description, and continued to characterize this type of woman as if it were common knowledge. How could he use the word "wife" in such a manner, and so matter-of-factly? Because this conversation was one that I had never had before with my husband, and he had never before spoken to me negatively about anyone's wife, I had to understand exactly what he meant by "dumpy and dowdy." I looked up these terms in Webster's Dictionary, and found that "dumpy" means "short and stout/fat," while "dowdy" means "no style; unattractively dressed." My understanding of his statement was confirmed.

I must admit that I had to catch my breath, as I was more than a little overwhelmed by the thought that maybe this is how my own husband saw me in my role as wife. Although I never saw myself as dumpy or dowdy, I would be lying if I didn't confess that I immediately went into the comparison mode many wives probably do when trying to determine the underlying reasons that husbands do the things they do and say some of the things they say; what's going on behind their words and actions?

I needed to understand how my husband's description of "wife" ran counter to that of a "girlfriend." Was this thing only about physical appearance, or was his description simply the tip of an iceberg? Was there something deeper and more significant, even pivotal, about how he perceived a "wife"? The thought alone made my temperature rise. I really wanted to punch back with some negative words. I felt the sting of that definition, and I took it personally. I decided, however, to take advantage of a learning opportunity, and to attempt to get the good (any good) that I could out of this situation.

I wondered if he really knew what he had said to me, and how deeply his words bored into me. Did he forget that he was no longer with the "boys" at the athletic tournament he attended that past weekend? Was he simply comfortable enough to say this to me, believing that it would not evoke any emotion, since he was describing someone else's wife? Nope; I took those words "looking like a wife, looking all dumpy and dowdy" as a direct insult to all wives, including me. I wondered what caused my husband to feel this way, and if other husbands and ex-husbands felt the same way.

At this time, as I said, however, my cooler, more collected self decided to turn the situation into a "win" for us wives, those of us who constantly seek to better understand our husbands, to improve our role as wives, and to maintain our relational confidence. This very real need comes into play for women, especially when our bodies have stopped responding to our words, wishes, and good intentions. Inevitably, we reach that point where we require some real (no, REAL) effort in order to achieve and maintain well-being. We have to exercise, and get proper nutrition to maintain that desired size, shape, and agility.

I set out on a new-found mission to obtain the answer to my questions. I began to seek out other husbands and ex-husbands, and even offered to have them respond by writing anonymous letters if doing so would foster a viable forum for honest dialogue. I sought to explore, uncover, and understand what husbands felt was needed in order to regain or maintain the "fire" in their marital relationships. Some husbands and ex-husbands did write letters, while others felt more comfortable responding to an anonymous survey or a live interview. The responses revealed so much more than I even thought to hope for. I expected to receive responses primarily centered on the physical attributes of wives. What I discovered is that there was this disparity between men's perceptions of wives and of girlfriends, but these men weren't talking about just any wife or any girlfriend. They really were concerned about "the one," the keeper.

It was all about the wife they had chosen, and the girlfriend she used to be during the courtship. Wow — This was another shocker for me! Although some admitted to having gone down that "forbidden" path, the husbands did not really want a mistress or a sidekick, or some different woman. They simply wanted back the girlfriend quality in their wives; you know, that fun-loving, physically attractive, patient, supportive, positive girlfriend that they married. They really did want the wife, but they wanted her as a girlfriend, too!

Why couldn't these husbands simply communicate their desires to their wives? Many did not want to risk the dreaded backlash, retaliation, or explosion that they feared might occur if husbands told their wives something as straightforward as "I would like it if you would lose some weight," or even a more gentle, "Let's start working out together." The results could be devastating on so many levels if a man tried to broach the subject, in any way, to call up the girlfriend that she used to be.

Let me ask you a question, reader. Can your husband be open with you about being a wife and a girlfriend, too? Would you like to know what that "rolled into one" concept means to the husbands that volunteered to speak up in my study? Walk with me.

Will this book save marriages? Maybe—maybe not. I'll be happy to "reach one," as they say, to teach even one. I have a feeling, though, that a lot more than a few women may be blessed by the considerations and conclusions of my study. Will it prevent infidelity? Maybe—maybe not. This book is not intended as a panacea for any marital issue. It is simply meant to stimulate a discussion between mates, a means to opening lines of communication, encouragement, and support; an open and honest discussion about what our husbands desire from us, as wives. My intent, for those of us who want to satisfy our man's "girlfriend" hunger, is for us to learn how wives can turn that man's desire into a win-win relationship, by reviving the inner girlfriend.

I have a theory about a woman being "market ready." This applies whether she is "on" the market or "in" the market, whether she is "looking," being looked at, or just "waiting" for the magic to happen. Not every woman is out on the "prowl," looking for Mr. Right, but all want to be on top of their game when he arrives. My theory applies whether yours is an "open-for-business" market, or you've already found the one and only who's allowed to shop there. My conclusions and suggestions apply whether you are still single, or you've already landed and married your dream guy.

Many single ladies seem to know that they have to be "Miss razzle, dazzle," or whatever it means for them, individually, to be the best they can be. But, you see, as a "market ready" wife you won't have to moan and groan, (unlike our sisters who choose not to be "market ready"), or ever have to get yourself "back" together by losing weight, going back to school, getting this, or giving up that. Forbid that, in the event that something goes awry in your marriage, your readiness scorecard comes up short. You, my sister-friend, as a woman living and breathing the "market ready" lifestyle, may, of course, have your good cry during a breakup (I wouldn't dare take that away), but then quickly lift your head and move on. It is completely up to you to have the choice of seamlessly slipping your fabulousness right back onto the market without agonizing over the fact that you have let yourself go.

Why land yourself in a place where you are unable to even lift your head past that tub of ice cream? Why let yourself fall into that slump where you have to claw your way into the direction of a sit up or a brisk walk? Breaking up is certainly not the goal here; if you're still reading, this is something we agree that we'd like to avoid. You understand my point. You can either focus on the negative at any point in a relationship and look for the fight or, you can see the potential for a positive win for everyone, no matter how your current or future relationship pans out. Are you in? Read on.

CHAPTER TWO

Why?

"There are those who look at things the way they are, and ask why... I dream of things that never were and ask why not?" - Robert Kennedy

The notion of any disparity or difference between being a girlfriend and a wife, in my husband's thinking, had never crossed my mind when we said "I do" on that beautiful summer day over sixteen years ago. I assumed, on that very day, when the minister pronounced us husband and wife, that my only responsibility to him, from now on, was to be a wife. You know what I mean, that "good thing" that the Bible says a man finds when he finds himself a wife.

It would have been easy to dismiss my husband's negative perception of that businessman's wife. I could have chalked it up to a passing moment's criticism, but I could not let it go without an attempt to discover the deeper significance behind it, the "why?" I thought that, if someone could be described as looking like a "wife," with such a cuttingly and categorically negative undertone, then what would conjure positive images, and invoke that spirit of "looking like a girlfriend?"

I took the word "looking" to relate to more than just physical appearance. The depth of the remark easily led me to take the posture that "looking like a wife" included the woman's behaviors, "actions, attitude, and appearance." Let's call it the "Triple A's."

Just in the interest of conducting a sort of "temperature check" as to whether there was something to be learned from my husband's statement, I initially questioned a few of my close male friends who were husbands or ex-husbands. Maybe I was simply being paranoid at this point in my marriage. I had to collect some data.

I asked, straight-out, if husbands and ex-husbands longed for their wives to exhibit more of the characteristics that they remembered during their time as girlfriends, or whether everything was just fine as time and changes went on in their relationships. Initially, some of these men appeared to rush toward the physical characterization of their wives, but, after some thought, they began to go deeper. I am not surprised that a woman's physical look stood out as a major point for many of the husbands/ex-husbands that chose to respond to my survey, or who volunteered to be interviewed. That's a given.

As I think back on what we, as a species, have known, even since Biblical times, the physical appearance and vitality of women, in terms of their relationships, was always clear. It was Bathsheba's beauty, spied from a window, which caught King David's eye. Queen Esther's beauty provided her the unprecedented privilege of an audience with King Xerxes, although she was uninvited, normally a move punishable by death. It was Sara's beauty that led to her husband Abraham lying to cover up, maintain, and protect their marital relationship, by saying that she was his sister. Beyond the likely good fortune of genetic beauty, these women modeled some significant characteristics that all women can learn from.

These great wives and women of history honored and respected their men. Sarah even referred to Abraham as "lord." Can you imagine how far Abraham's chest must have been sticking out to know that his woman freely and sincerely gave him this kind of respect? It is that respect, in the traditional sense, that Otis Redding espoused when he wrote and recorded the original version of the song *Respect*, later made famous by Aretha Franklin. Redding desired to receive a "little respect when he got home." Franklin's focus was somewhat different. She added sexual innuendo with her recitation of "Sock it to me!" as part of the lyrics. Redding's respect was more aligned with that stated in Ephesians 5:33 (NIV) which provides that "...each one of you also must love his wife as he loves himself, and the wife must respect her husband." This requirement of respect is clear. As I heard Dr. Tony Evans, (Senior Pastor of Oak Cliff Bible Fellowship) say, in one of his sermons, "Men are moved mentally, while you move a woman through her heart." Don't you agree? Most of us girls are emotional creatures, heart-focused, to some extent, while men begin their focus with the eye. So it's no surprise that women's priority is love. For men, the high seat goes to respect.

Dr. Evans' statement is consistent with what I deduced from my interviews, letters, and survey. When I tore away all of the "outside noise," I found that husbands and ex-husbands simply want most to feel honored and respected, both by how his woman treats him, and how she treats herself. Not one participant said they only wanted the "love" that a wife showed during her incumbency as girlfriend. Could it be that when men feel honored and respected, in these ways, that they feel loved? Are those womanly attributes and virtues of the desirable wife and desirable girlfriend equally important in a man's eye? Is a significant part of what a man perceives as honor and respect attributable to a two-pronged focus from his mate, how their wives treat them, and how they honor and present themselves?

When you think about it, this should all be common knowledge, shouldn't it? Nevertheless, it bodes some introspection and self-analysis. I did not roll my eyes at this whole honor/respect notion, because it aligns with biblical teachings where wives are instructed to honor and respect their husbands. I realize that there is no mention there of love, at all.

I was determined to give husbands and ex-husbands the opportunity to voice their opinions and desires. I must admit that some of what I heard was difficult to swallow and digest, but I decided to put on my big girl shorts and hold on for the ride. Since some of us women believe that men, in general, don't communicate their true feelings as it relates to our relationships, I wanted to ensure that I gave the proper space so that men could speak and have their relational truth heard.

Join me as I address some of the major findings and themes of the feedback I received via letters, interviews, and survey results. If you are one who would like to unearth that buried "girlfriend" again, and you want to revive your "market readiness," then you should jump aboard this train with an open mind. Remember that this is all about creating a "win-win." Some ask why bother? This journey may not be for you! Come along if you answer that person with the question, "Why would you not?" My marriage is worth the expedition. How about you?

CHAPTER THREE

Communication: Two Parts Listening; One Part Speaking

"I know you believe you understand what you think I said, but I am not sure you realize that what you heard is not what I meant." - Robert McCloskey

ANONYMOUS HUSBAND LETTER #1:

Dear Wife,

Can I please have some Jell-O? Some time ago, you asked me what I wanted for dessert and I told you Jell-O, but you went the extra mile and made a wonderful red velvet cake. Another day you asked me and I gave the same answer. Once again, you went above and beyond by presenting me with an incredible blackberry cobbler topped with French vanilla ice cream. Obviously, you have the skills to make it happen so why can't I get some Jell-O?

This seems to be a common theme with us. I ask for something simple — you far exceed it — but I'm not completely satisfied. I might just ask for a little quiet time with you. You feel that you cook, clean, work, take care of the kids, gave me a son, do the laundry, and a million other superwoman things — you are taking care of me. I really appreciate all those <u>things,</u> but what about <u>me</u>? Those things are duties, but "Jell-O" is personal!

This might sound stupid, but men don't see the big picture, just the immediate goal. I didn't notice the music, the atmosphere, or how you were dressed. However, I did notice the absence of "Jell-O."

Much Love,

The husband who wrote "Anonymous Husband Letter #1" appears frustrated by his wife's failure to provide the "Jell-O" that he requested from her. We all understand that this husband is not literally seeking Jell-O, a product on supermarket shelves; whatever "Jell-O" represents for him, he is not getting it from his wife. There appears to be a communication gap and an emotional disconnect. They are speaking to one another, but the message has gotten lost in transmission or translation. The wife clearly believes that she is surpassing what her husband wants, and that going beyond his request is a good thing. Right? Wrong! The husband wants what he wants, nothing more, nothing less. He has requested "Jell-O" repeatedly. No matter how simple and unexciting it may appear to the wife, this is what HE wants. Maybe the husband described his desire as "Jell-O" to symbolize to his wife just how simple it would be to please him. "Jell-O" is way less complicated than red velvet cake and blackberry cobbler. So why is the wife unable to grasp this and understand that giving him what he wants may mean less work for her in the end? You see, when a wife fails to give her husband what he wants, in favor of what SHE believes is best for him, the husband may get frustrated, and (guess what!)

seek to find his "Jell-O" somewhere else. Big surprise! How can we wives zone in on our husbands' "Jell-O" desires? I'm assuming that you're still reading because this IS what you want for your marriage.

As I look back, I realize that I have personally experienced a failure to communicate period with my husband. I thought that I was doing a great job as a wife and mother until one day, during a tense discussion with my husband, he said that, while he thought I was doing a great job as a mother, that I appeared to over-focus on the mothering, leaving him out, and not adequately fulfilling my role as a wife.

Digging deeper, I was not sure that it was as simple as something in my "role as a wife" that he was missing. I realized that it was in my role as girlfriend that I had become remiss, that part of me that made him feel confident, honored, and secure in our relationship. He said that he wanted to be reunited with the person he saw in me before motherhood came along and stole my focus. What? I admit that I thought I did a great job at multi-tasking, and, as far as I was concerned, that included my role as wife. It was quite surprising to hear that I had failed by classifying my responsibility as a wife in the same category as my other responsibilities of mothering, cooking, grocery shopping, and work. Heck, I had mistakenly assumed that every responsibility I had after marriage amounted to my being a wife. Had I completely lost touch, and so soon after saying, "I do"? Could this be the reason some husbands seek their fulfillment elsewhere, not necessarily with another woman, but even with other things? The look in his eyes and the emotion in his voice touched my heart, and caused me to truly listen. I listened with more than my ears; I also listened with my eyes, and with an open heart. The resultant connection caused me to truly feel the depth of my husband's desire.

Also, through my canvassing of other husbands, my husband's feelings were validated. Could we be misinterpreting our husbands' desires?

I have to admit that I initially thought the "Jell-O" seeking husband was asking for sex, and my thinking was that if that is what he wants, why didn't he simply say, "I WANT SEX!" Out of my own selfishness I initially sided with the wife and thought that if she doesn't know what her husband's "Jell-O" represents, then apparently, it is he that has failed to effectively communicate with her, because it is he that has the unrequited desire.

I digress... again. We all know that we women take on a lot of responsibility when we marry. We feel a sense of responsibility for the direction of the lives of our children and what is best for them, but, somewhere down the line (and this is important ladies), we start to feel this same type of responsibility for our husbands. We moved from the dating period, when we believed these men could handle anything, to the married period, believing we have to decide what is best for them — like a child. Could the wife's desire to give the husband what she thinks he needs versus what he desires, be a sign that her emotional prong may be in need of some retuning in order to bring her girlfriend mode back into balance? Sometimes our choosing to "fix" things in others may be a signal for us to turn the attention inward to determine if what we are doing is really about our desire to serve our husbands or a way for us to ignore what we should be working on within ourselves.

This is where I believe we set ourselves on the path to failure. We make a wrong turn at some juncture when a path called "Connectedness and Allure," a place where we are emotionally connected to our husbands, turns off onto the downhill road called "Matron's Cove," a dead end, or worse, a sheer drop where we lose the sensuousness in our marriages becoming more like mothers to our husbands instead of wives. Could our lack of confidence in our husbands, whether overtly or covertly displayed, have an effect on our girl friendliness? Does this wrong turn become a grim prognosis for the honor and respect that men thrive on? I believe it does, because this imbalance affects the core of our relationship, and of our whole being. So, here we are: What can we do to recover and rehabilitate our communication with our mates? How do we regain that emotional balance within ourselves that gives us the freedom to be open to receiving instead of being on-guard and unable to receive or decipher what is being communicated? Sometimes I can't hear the true message being delivered by my husband because of my emotional state which sometimes causes me to hear things, negative things, he did not say or mean. Regaining that emotional balance might require some "me" time, a spa visit or even counseling. While we each may have to take different paths to regain our emotional balance, our goal is still the same...to get it back to the point where our emotional state benefits our relationships with our husbands and helps us regain our market ready status.

D I S C U S S I O N :

Let's assume that it was your husband who wrote this anonymous letter. (One of your husbands did.) Take some thoughtful time and write down some recollections of your husband having repeatedly requested something from you, the same thing, on more than one occasion. What was the time, place, atmosphere, and, more importantly, your emotional state? These all play a role in deciphering what may have seemed a non-issue to you, the all-important what his "Jell-O" represents:

_____

_____

_____

_____

_____

_____

Did your husband directly communicate his Jell-O desire to you, or did it come, rather, as a negative comment or some other form of communication? In essence, did you give him one thing of your choosing, and he rejected it without telling you exactly what it was that he wanted?

If you feel that your husband is afraid to be open with you about something he truly wants from you, then, before you begin probing his "Jell-O" desire, talk to him with patience and compassion. Make him feel safe enough to really tell you exactly what he wants. I assume you still know how to help him to release his pent up energy, right? Sometimes husbands may be yearning for a "fantasy" experience, but believe their wives may find it childish or outlandish. Consequently, they have a fear of letting their wives know what's on their minds. Unfortunately, for whatever consequences may come, a husband may even seek that fantasy fulfillment somewhere else. These yearnings are powerful.

I heard one minister-husband liken the satisfaction he got from his wife to the great food being served at several restaurants where he loved to dine. He said that one day he left home heading to church after eating a great meal that his wife prepared for him at home. During his trip across town he passed several restaurants that served great food, but did not need to stop, he said, because he was not hungry. His wife had fed him well before he left home. He had no reason to stop anywhere else to eat. Do you get my point? Are you satisfying your husband's hunger, or forcing him to eat out? Hmmm …

Consider the benefits of letting your husband know (and meaning it) that you are willing to have an unguarded, "yes, I am truly listening," conversation with no ramifications or strings attached. Consider what you have to gain when you are open to hearing his heart's desires. You may or may not do whatever it is he describes, but at least you are open to letting him talk about it. Who knows what lovely compromise might arise. Once he's got that out in the open, you may be able to find a happy medium that gives him whatever breakthrough he needs, as well as a sense of honor, respect, and love from you. A bonus comes to you in that, in the process, you get a sense of emotional satisfaction, and deepened connectedness — the knowing that he has been fulfilled, and that he doesn't have to go sit at some other table.

Give yourself some time to work through this process, as it will certainly not come naturally for most, or overnight. You must have had the magic on that day when he said, "I do," and you can continue to have the magic. If you want to move back into your "girlfriend" mode, you must be open to the adventure of rediscovering what your husband's "Jell-O" desire represents. Don't force a freeze in your relationship like the wife mentioned in the letter. This temporary lull that comes as a season in relationships brings to mind the Ashford and Simpson song (you know the one?) where there is a discussion between mates, and the husband is attempting to communicate to his wife the fact that the things she used to do or say don't happen anymore. The man in the song doesn't know how to bring up the subject, though, saying, "It seems like such a funny thing to talk about." Finally, he asks her the question that has been burning deep in his psyche "Is it still good to ya?" he sings.

CHAPTER FOUR

Can You Handle The Truth?

*"The naked truth is always better than
the best-dressed lie." - Ann landers*

I personally interviewed husbands and ex-husbands
who preferred to speak with me rather than to write
anonymous letters or to participate in the anonymous survey. I enjoyed, not only listening to the message conveyed by these husbands and ex-husbands,
but the emotions, comparisons, and gestures accom-
panying it all. One interviewee was an ex-husband
whom I have personally known for over 30 years. I
can confidently say that he's a man who truly makes
the effort to follow the commandments of Christ. He
also is a lifelong athlete, a professional, and an intel-
lectual rolled into one, so getting his feedback was
invaluable to me.

I must begin with my conclusion concerning my conversation with Interviewee #1…I was shocked! In my 30+ years of knowing him, I never heard him speak so directly and pointedly about this notion of a wife as a girlfriend. He immediately focused on the physical aspects. As he put it, not leaving out his biblical connection, "If a man finds a good thing when he finds a wife, then why would she not take care of that good thing?" I assumed he wasn't really expecting a response from me, since I was conducting the interview. He went further, stating that he compares the physical attributes of a wife to that of a new house. I assume a brick house. He said, "If you buy a new house, would you allow the toilet to remain stopped up or broken down? No! Of course not." He answered his own question. He said, "Why would you allow yourself to become broken down, in essence, stopped up?" Ironically, as we went further in the conversation, he revealed some real justifications behind his reasoning. Just as folks admire nice houses, I believe that he, on some level, loved the attention he received when folks admired his brick house of a wife. He even confirmed my assumption by saying that he wanted his wife to be that lady mentioned in the song "The Men All Pause," by the

R&B group Klymaxx, wherein a line of the lyrics say, "The men all paused when I walked into the room." Another great piece of information for my fellow wives. Some of our husbands desire us to look good for them, but also for their friends. Really? Really!

Anonymous Husband Letter #2 and Anonymous Husband Letter #3 seem to bear out this interesting point. Don't get me wrong; when I use the term "brick house" to describe our bodies you must understand that like brick houses that we live in, they are of different shapes and sizes. There isn't simply one model type of a "brick house". Your focus, as wives, is not to be the brick house that you see in another woman, but that brick house that you know you initially built as the Market Ready Sister/Market Ready Soul mate. Just as a brick house needs maintenance in order to remain in pristine condition, the same goes for our bodies. Are you maintaining your body giving it the proper nutrition, exercise, rest and care necessary to keep it in pristine condition? That is, getting your physical prong back to where you desire it to be in your quest to regain and retain your market ready status. Just like some of us hire services to maintain the houses we live in, don't overlook using some outside assistance to help you maintain your physical house. Do you need to hire a personal trainer, get some friends together to run a 5K or half marathon, or take some sort of cleansing class or treatments to rid yourself of those food addictions?

We really have no excuses not to have our houses in order. We have too many resources readily available. In January 2000, I took a cleanse class after having difficulty breathing and not understanding why I was being prescribed Prednisone. The cleanse class was a three week raw food cleanse which was a shock to me because I not only loved eating food, but cooked food. So the path, for me, began with the notion of not eating chicken or turkey and then not eating something cooked made me think this was going to be the longest three weeks of my life. It has been thirteen years since I took that first cleanse class and I am still cleansing and feeling fantastic with the side benefit of having my physical structure in girlfriend mode. The point of telling you this is to encourage you to seek out the resources that work for you. I needed the cleanse class because it allowed me to eliminate the Prednisone, eliminate foods that were not agreeing with my system and to drop a few pounds in the process, all for a healthier me.

ANONYMOUS HUSBAND LETTER #2

Dear Wife,

Even today, you are the woman of my dreams. I love the way you smile and carry yourself; I always have, and still do. You are highly intelligent, regal in your walk, feminine as a rose, voluptuous, with a beautiful sense of humor (and you even laugh at my dry jokes). You are also a godly woman. I talk the spiritual — you walk the spiritual. I have learned how to love unconditionally through your example.

I truly love you, but over the past few years I sometime wonder, do you still love yourself? Do you value yourself enough to take the time to take that walk, to choose holistic health over detrimental delicacies, to love yourself for you and not for me or any external reasons? Do you TAKE TIME to love on yourself (even when the budget does not allow) … like driving to a park, taking time to rejuvenate? … TAKING TIME to "peel off" the wilting petals, and allowing yourself to come into full bloom?

This is the "groove" I pray that you get back, because that was your flow and halo. As a husband, sometimes I feel guilty and ask myself, "Did I take the glow away?" But after much prayer the Lord has assured me that I have to let go of that guilt. He said "No it's not your fault, because you were not the one that gave her that glow. It is out of your control, so step back, and give her space. I am waiting on her to come to me for this restoration, renewal, and refreshing. I am her fountain of youth! " (See, Isaiah 40:31).

Let me be clear: I do not want a showcase wife, but I do want to see you present yourself in all that God has called and created you to be… your best self in all the glory that God has put inside you, letting your light shine brightly. My prayer is that you stop trying to tame your wild beauty that was not meant to be tamed. Stop trying to make palatable to others what <u>was</u> meant to be out of control — beyond self-imposed limitations and societal, legalistic, and cultural boundaries … (Be who you are) black, beautiful and bubbling over. In the words of a favorite '70s tune, "Let the rain fall down upon her—she's a sweet and gentle flower growing wild."

Yeah, that's my woman. I see you blooming perennially. It's your season. It's your time (and I can't wait to get you back)! How do you make a grown man cry? When his woman is loosed!!!

Love,

Anonymous Husband Letter #2 is the best endorsement I could receive to advocate for wives being market ready, and of the rewards women get for giving husbands much needed and sought after respect. What is so heartwarming, to me, about this letter is that the husband is saying that when you "love on yourself," the husband also gets some of the benefits of that self-love ... a better, emotional, financial, physical, professional, and spiritual partner. In addition, the husband feels respected by how the wife treats herself; poor treatment equals less respect. This husband is communicating that when the wife fails to be a mate who is market ready, it causes him angst. It is so emotional for him that it appears he wants to impress on his wife that when she is loosed from negative energies and fetters, he also is loosed, thereby confirming what we have already surmised. The wife's "market readiness" strongly affects her husband, and, subsequently, their mutual relationship.

This all lines up biblically: In Mark 10:8 (NIV), it says "the two shall become one flesh." Consequently, if the wife is either doing something that is not in her own best interest, or moving in a positive direction, naturally it affects her husband. This husband yearns to have back that girlfriend that he proposed to.

What has stolen her focus? Did she use to do things that excited him, but now has become predictable and boring? This husband wondered aloud if he had stolen the excitement his wife once exhibited. No. The wife has to first decide that she wants to recon-figure her positive attributes or shed the layers of responsibility that she has allowed to glaze over who she really is beneath it all. I know some of us wives believe that once we get the children out of the house and pay off the bills, we will return to being that hot number we used to be. The reality is that sometimes life doesn't wait for you to return to your best self. Life moves on.

DISCUSSION:

As I got older, and, eventually, more wise, I believed some of the things I did and the sexy clothes I wore had to take a back seat to this supposedly more mature, professional and refined person I believed I had become. What I discovered, however, was that my husband still desired my "girlfriend" look, especially in our personal, private time. He didn't want to live on memories alone of those sexy clothes and that woman he fell for. Huh? Initially I would have never thought such a thing. I guess Ashford and Simpson said it best when they sang, "There's nothing like the real thing baby." We wives have to continue to consider how our husbands are stimulated. While I believe, like others, that successful marriages may hinge on having "amnesia" about some things that have occurred in the relationship, let's not get it twisted. Let go of what weighs the relationship down, not what gives it joy. There is certainly nothing to be gained when the wife determines to have "amnesia" about those things she did in the beginning to please her husband. Think back. What did you use to do? What did you give him, emotionally, spiritually and physically, that you may have stopped giving today and need to reignite? From a sensuality standpoint, there are plenty of resources and almost unlimited creative ways to turn up the heat with your husband from an emotional, physical and yes, spiritual perspective. I acknowledge that one of the most sensual, intimately suggestive resources I have found is the Bible. Yes, the Bible. I recall the sensuous love of a husband and wife as they speak to each other in Song of Songs 7: 8-10 (KJV). Let's open our eyes and see what they are truly saying to each other through the imagery:

> "... I said, I will go up to the palm tree, I will take hold of the boughs thereof now also thy breasts shall be as clusters of the vine and the smell of thy nose like apples and the roof of thy mouth like the best wine for my beloved that goeth down sweetly, causing the lips of those that are asleep to speak. I am my beloveds and his desire is toward me."

Now you must admit that is hot and biblical, too! Yes, God ordained sensuality! "Why did she go there?" you might be asking yourself. Well, it is because some of our fellow wives, who have some marital years under their belts, sometimes become so holy that they forget the sensuality that once drove their husbands to them. How easy it is to forget that it *IS* being holy when you fulfill that role. Let this be a gentle reminder that you can give your husband something he can feel, and still honor and serve the Lord. Hallelujah, everybody!

ANONYMOUS HUSBAND LETTER # 3

Dear Wife,

When I met you, we became good friends, and that is something we still maintain. Being friends allows me to tell you the truth about anything, and for you to do the same. When I met you, you wore a size six (6), and I will not accept a one in front of that six (a size 16). I'm not trying to say you have to stay the same, but please exercise and look good to me, because if I stop caring about how you look, we will have a problem. It's just nice to see you looking good and turning heads when you enter a room.

Also, I love an independent woman who can make decisions when I'm not around. This is a partnership, not a sole proprietorship. Making time for me is important, too. You are a great mother; my daughter could not have a better mom, but you shouldn't forget about being my wife. It's nice when married people can have time alone, and just be married, not parents all the time. However, at the end of the day, I just want to be respected, cherished, and loved.

Love,

DISCUSSION:

Sometimes I wonder if some husbands want their wives to look good for the shot in the arm it gives to the husband's ego and the boost to his social rank among his male friends. Interviewee #1 appears to be aligned and co-signed with the sentiments of the husband who penned Anonymous Husband Letter #3. As another husband expresses his desire to have other men pause when his wife enters the room, I'm thinking that this must be a male thing. I never heard any of my girlfriends express a desire to have every woman turn around with a "wow" when their husbands enter the room. We women, to tell the truth, really would prefer that the women not get excited about our men, and that they keep their eyes down or face some other direction when our men enter the room. We really don't want other women pumping up our husbands' egos. I guess this is another point where wives differ from husbands.

I readily admit that each year it really is more difficult to keep my body at the peak level I desire, let alone maintain the fierceness that my husband desires. It would be easy for me to turn the mirror on my husband and say that he too, just like some other husbands we notice (eyes up and fully forward), faces the difficulty of maintaining that optimum physique. Since this is not a book about pointing fingers, however, I continue with the goal in mind of making things better through my own actions and I hope you will do the same.

I have learned that if I want something different, I have to do something different. Here I am now in weight lifting class, kick boxing, and running half marathons, which, let me tell you is not an easy commitment, but the workout is worth the work. It leaves me feeling both emotionally and physically great, after all is said and done. Well, I guess I can say it helps to keep me feeling and being market ready. So, while my husband may benefit from the after-effects of my efforts, I too benefit on various levels: physically, emotionally, and spiritually. The time

I spend pushing my body also helps to clear my mind and lift my spirits. That is an absolute win for me, too.

If you look deeper into this letter written by Anonymous Husband #3, you see in his ending that he states that all he wants is to feel "respected, cherished and loved." That respect thing runs deep. Again, how does it connect so easily in a man's mind with a woman's physical attributes? I am going to assume that the woman's physical make-up must only be part of the formula that makes a husband feel respected. Truth be told, I have seen some wives who put the "brick" in "brick house" when it comes to physical presentation,, and yet the husband is screaming for a divorce. He's saying nasty things about her in the media, based on something that was missing: she was not giving him some component to make him feel respected. Therefore, I surmise that the husband wants to be respected and that the wife, in several ways, communicates respect. One way, too often overlooked by women, is how she treats and presents herself.

Has your husband ever directly or indirectly criticized anything about your physical appearance? Did he do it indirectly, by being overly complimentary about the body of some television or movie star, or other public personality? If so, how did you receive his message? At some level of reflection, was he correct? I am on board for physical exercise that contributes to my health and longevity... I easily get that. I find it hard, though, to ever say to other women, and let alone myself, to get physically in shape for your husband. I believe you get in shape for yourself and allow your husband the benefit of basking in your glow. When it comes to getting and keeping myself on track physically, I find it easier to set a goal with my own well-being in mind. Completing a marathon, half-marathon, 5-K, kick boxing class or a raw cleanse, all give me something to shoot for. Simply saying that I want to get in shape doesn't excite me and leaves me with a multitude of excuses for continuously falling off the wagon. You know what you need to do. You don't need anyone else to highlight it for you. Be honest about where you are and where you want to go and just do it! But do it for yourself.

CHAPTER FIVE

You Have Power

*"In every marriage more than a week old,
there are grounds for divorce. The trick
is to find, and continue to find, grounds
for marriage." -Robert Anderson*

I was excited and looking forward to my talk with Interviewee #2. This participant is 70+ years old, with the look of a man much younger, both facially and physically. He is the father of one of my colleagues. After hearing my colleague describe her father as a man who dated women even younger than she is, and as a man who eventually married a woman half his age, I definitely wanted to peek inside his world. I wondered what golden nuggets of wisdom I might extract to help me and other wives.

After obtaining confirmation to contact Interviewee #2, I dialed his phone number and, when he picked up, I became somewhat nervous, because the energy in his voice made him sound like a much younger man, yet I knew that he was the father of a colleague. He was expecting my call. I delved right into my topic, explaining the goal of my interview, and informing him that I wanted to determine whether husbands and ex-husbands missed the girlfriend they had in their wives before asking them to marry.

He cut me off and interjected "Y'all have the control because y'all have the pocket book.' At first I had no clue what he was saying, so I responded, "Excuse me?" He repeated himself, as if hearing it again would make it clearer. "Y'all have the pocket-book." I repeated the word twice quietly to myself, "Pocketbook, pocketbook" hoping that something would click, and that I would finally understand what he was trying to say. After I got past the fact that a man 70+ years old could be thinking sexually, I finally understood his euphemism. I said "Oh, you mean ..." Yes, that's what he meant. He was saying that since we women have certain anatomical attractions that appeal to men, that we, in essence, controlled the relationship. Really? I thought I was doing well with understanding the physical aspect of what men crave. Now, I wonder if that optimum physical quality is necessary because it adds to the beauty of the "pocketbook" that Interviewee #2 describes in such an unvarnished manner. So, I must ask my fellow wives, what we are doing to add value to the "pocketbook?"

ANONYMOUS HUSBAND LETTER #4

Dear Wife,

I will never forget the first time you cooked for me. I came to your apartment. You were made up, with a pretty dress and pearls. You prepared a great five-course meal (and even cracked open a can of Chunky Clam Chowder), and we had dinner by candlelight. After dinner and dessert, you changed into lingerie and treated me very special.

Frankly, I thought I had hit the lottery! I got a looker, a cooker, and a little freak. What more could a brother like me ask for?

That was a memorable experience. Unfortunately, you turned out not to be the cooker, or the freak you portrayed that evening. In fact, the next time I saw candles, our electricity was cut off. For a long time I felt like a sucker, hoodwinked, bamboozled, misled. It was as if Monty Hall tricked me with one of those misleading hints. "Behind door number two is a brand new two-seater vehicle," he bellows. Then they roll out a dog sled.

I guess that the lesson here should be an easy one: "Whatever you do to get him is what you have to do to keep him."

Love,

DISCUSSION:

Simply put, this husband feels like his wife tricked him into marriage. He thought he was getting one thing, only to end up getting something far less desirable. This, my sisters, is not a way to start or to maintain a marriage. While this example is extreme, I wonder if other husbands who wish to have their girlfriends back also, on some level, believe that they have been hoodwinked. I'm just sayin'. Let's take a cold, hard look at ourselves, ladies ... me included! Have you transformed so much that your husband doesn't even see a resemblance to the person he married?

Just as in Anonymous Husband Letter #2, it appears that this husband (#4) wants to shed tears (of joy) in a fulfilling marriage. Is the exciting person he remembers hiding behind the "dowdy" wife façade described by my husband? Or, as some husbands who took the anonymous survey (which is discussed later) believe, has child rearing leaped into first place for the wife's attention? Are you more excited about preparing something for the PTA bake sale than cooking up something hot for your husband?

I am one who doesn't dispute the notion that "what it took to get him is what you have to do to keep him," but sometimes I wonder if we need to ask at what cost. I have heard your complaint that some husbands seem to highlight shortcomings, never fully appreciating all that you do to raise your children (You're working a full-time job, reviewing homework, meeting with teachers, playing chauffeur, etc.), and maintain the house and yourself. Having to confront any negativity from your mate when you count yourself thoroughly invested, can throw even the best athlete off her game. I do want to be quick to make no excuses for this disappointing behavior, or for our penchant for throwing out the baby with the bath water. When you feel like your spouse is clipping your wings with negativity, you must resist the urge to let yourself be bogged down by what can become a sinking ship, especially if you simply stand by and watch without remembering your win-win goal of becoming market ready. Continuously see yourself in that market ready mode, and work to make it your reality. Being market ready will give you that extra energy and confidence that you will need so, if at any point in your marriage you need to fly away with a "broken wing," as a Martina McBride song so aptly puts it, you will have built up the strength to do it. I believe, however, that when your husband sees your regained market ready state, he will think twice. You know what I mean.

ANONYMOUS HUSBAND LETTER #5

Dear wife,

As the twilight years are bringing a close to our [lives and a] long and loving marriage, I have begun to reflect on how our union has prospered through the different eras of the black family crisis. When we took our marriage vows at a famous black Baptist church in the mid 1950's, our love toward one another never faltered under the best or worst of circumstances. The unwavering human emotion of love through the years served as a foundation of mutual respect for each other.

Being married during America's "Jim Crow" era compelled us to set aside petty marital disagreements in order to overcome being second class citizens. The development of a solid social network from day one with close family ties and friends has contributed heavily to avoiding a "Tiger Woods" type scenario in our long and prosperous marriage. Attending numerous social events together, including fraternity dances and other social galas helped us avoid slipping into to the dull marriage trap.

As the 21st century gains momentum, the black divorce and out of wedlock birth statistics continue to go through the roof, because of the absence of love and true marital commitment. I take pride in knowing that our love became stronger as the years went by! More importantly, we still like each other 24 hours a day. Thanks wife for a long and prosperous marriage!

Sincerely,

ST

DISCUSSION:

While some of the husbands who were interviewed, wrote a letter and/or completed the survey appear to find reasons that would justify parting ways, this husband writing the Anonymous Husband Letter #5 appears to have found the reason for him and his wife to stay together. Their love has bonded and remained close as they, as a team, have continually found ways to strengthen their marital bond. Like any nicely heated relationship, they have tended to their fire, and have not allowed the flame to go out in their marriage. Their relationship proclaims the message that if you want to keep the flame going in your marriage, somebody has to be willing to strike the match and find a way to keep fanning the flames. What are you doing to keep the fire blazing in your marriage?

CHAPTER SIX

Do The Right Thing

"It's the action, not the fruit of the action, that's important. You have to do the right thing. It may not be in your power, may not be in your time, that there'll be any fruit. But that doesn't mean you stop doing the right thing. You may never know what results come from your action. But if you do nothing, there will be no result."— <u>Mahatma Gandhi</u>

ANONYMOUS HUSBAND LETTER #6

Dear Wife,

The whole time we dated, it was never a mystery that I was going to get the panties. Then we got married, and suddenly I had to build up points to get some. And the points didn't come easily. It was like collecting S&H Green Stamps, back in the day. "... gave mother-in-law a compliment, plus 10 stamps; cleaned the room, plus 5 stamps; left the toilet seat up minus 15 stamps." And don't discount world events coming into play. "The Celtics lost. I'm not in the mood." "No, I don't want to, because I feel so bad about the oil spill in the Gulf Coast." "No, not tonight. The Steve Harvey show was cancelled."

It can't be a good thing to make a man feel like he has to work too hard for something that so many ladies are willing to give away. In fact, it isn't good for anyone to start thinking of intimacy as a commodity. If you do, you will eventually think about return on investment, and how to diversify your portfolio. Besides, who wants to feel like their mate is doing them a favor? Personally, I thought our intimacy was the one thing I was good at!

It would be great to know, after competing all day at work that I don't have to compete in my home, constantly tallying points in order to earn legitimacy and affection.

Love,

Like this wife of Anonymous Husband # 6, have you attempted to train your husband like Pavlov's dog? Do you use your "pocketbook" as the treat you throw at him when he does exactly what you want, and then you deny the treat when you don't get what you want? As the husband intimates above, you can't bargain over what you should be giving to your husband as a free-will gift. When you do that, you run the risk of having him dine somewhere else where the price he has to pay is much lower and, in some instances, free, with no strings attached.

I understand wives who say that they have so much on their plates that they are too tired for sex some days. That's where understanding your husband's "Jell-O" pays off. Ask yourself whether you are going beyond what your husband desires, setting unrealistic, even mythical standards, and tiring yourself out, when you could simply give him the "Jell-O" he desires and be done instantly just like the Jell-O product. You might save some time and energy for yourself, and make your mate happy, too.

CHAPTER SEVEN

The Whole Truth

*"Coming together is a beginning; keeping together
is progress; working together is success."*
-Henry Ford

Even after receiving letters and engaging in conversations with husbands and ex-husbands which more than answered the original question of whether husbands wanted their wives as girlfriends too, I refused to accept it. I made excuses, convincing myself that I needed greater confirmation of my earlier findings. I decided that conducting a brief and anonymous survey would be the key. In a selfish kind of way, I thought that a survey conducted with more respondents would refute or, at a minimum, diminish the veracity of the earlier messages, and make wives feel comfortable about where we are in the current state of our marriages. Do you suppose, as I initially did, that the husbands and ex-husbands who wrote the letters and gave the interviews/comments were an anomaly? If your answer is yes, I suggest you reconsider, as the anonymous survey results that were received bear out that the letter writers and interviewees were consistent in their focus, not reflective of any one man on an island with isolated views. A variety and diversity of men in the marital arena appear to have similar and ongoing yearnings, and, in some respects, frustrations.

After receiving some initial feedback, I barreled toward my central point of seeking to discover what, if anything, these husbands/ex-husbands found to be missing from their wives and/or in their marriages, and what they believed were the reasons behind it. I wasn't pushing to the point of seeking a long list of things that would prompt those not already divorced to run out and get one, but pushing them back to the place where they were excited about asking that certain woman to be their wife. While many agreed that the woman they married was not the same woman today, nor the marriage at the same highpoint as when it began, I prodded for the "why"? Why do you believe your wife/ex-wife fails/failed to display her premarital self and what absent factors do you or did you desire to have back in your wife and/or marriage to bring them back to that highpoint? The top responses given as to why their wife failed to display her premarital self, included: 1. Career/Financial pressures, 2. Her attitude changed, and 3. She gained substantial weight. While the notion of these categories bothered me somewhat, especially considering all that we wives do in support of our homes and marriages, after sitting down and doing some thoughtful reflection, I realized that when you peel away all of the exterior noises, these men were simply saying they miss the "girlfriend" in their wives. You see, when I put these three categories up against the five prongs (emotional, financial, physical, professional and spiritual) of a Market Ready Sister/Market Ready Soul mate (i.e. girlfriend), I find that they are clearly encompassed therein. Hooray! Clarity, at last! As you can see, being market ready (that girlfriend again) continues to be a win-win for both husbands and wives.

I did not stop upon learning that our husbands/ex-husbands also, in a roundabout way, were advocating for our being market ready. I needed more from them and in their own words, uncut and unedited. I, therefore, did not edit the list, although I have concerns. Some items are redundant, some unclear, and some – downright pedestrian. Nevertheless, the survey gave them that opportunity and they took it by giving wives/ex-wives more than eighty recommendations to reignite the girlfriend in them and/or help restore/reinforce our marriages. While you likely will not agree with all of the recommendations, try reading them with an open mind and with the goal of better understanding why these men feel the way they do. Apparently, something has triggered them to recommend the following considerations to us:

1. *Appreciation.*
2. *Patience and less anger.*
3. *We were close. I thought we were a team.*
4. *No "expectations" that set me up for failure.*
5. *Future thinking instead of past performance.*
6. *Spiritual attraction (somehow my judgmental attitude knocked this out of her).*
7. *Child-like fearlessness (ready to do bolder things).*
8. *No overthinking the relationship, which suppresses sex.*
9. *One day at a time.*
10. *Take off the makeup and show your true self.*
11. *Remember how much you loved him.*

12. *Trust, don't question.*

13. *Be spontaneous.*

14. *Occasionally make your man feel like he is still the hero, the knight in shining armor and the perfect man for you (that you thought he was when you were dating).*

15. *Men want to know that they are still the guy you would marry again.*

16. *Stop trying to protect yourself and help your husband lead.*

17. *Don't use passive aggressive tactics to steer the ship, even if it is headed in a direction you don't desire. Question the direction in a respectful way, similar to approaching a foreign dignitary.*

18. *Trust God that He will steer the ship in the right direction, even if the man isn't going there.*

19. *Partner with your man instead of trying to "set" the direction.*

20. *Remain faithful to God despite the husband's lack of faithfulness.*

21. *Remove negative assumptions (assume innocence).*

22. *Add grace, mercy, love and kindness daily.*

23. *Remove selfishness and lust for more material things.*

24. *Believe in God's way.*

25. *Keep up your appearance.*

26. *As the jar of life fills up, save space for time with just you and your spouse.*

27. *Always go back to the initial dating.*

28. *Be honest — honest with yourself most of all about what you want and expect from a guy. A relationship is about compromise, not just love.*

29. *Do the same things it took to get your man, to keep your man.*

30. *Communicate and don't listen to single friends or non-Christians if you both are active Christians.*

31. *As we get older, remember who you were when you met; some things can't be controlled. We all mature at a different rate.*

32. *Talk, do not yell, argue or be controlling.*

33. *Have discussions and weather disagreements; compromise does not mean that you get your way all the time.*

34. *Always flirt. Show that you like him; not always leading to sex.*

35. *Be his friend, maybe not best friend, understanding that he may have a best friend other than you.*

36. *Try to understand what makes your partner tick.*

37. *Don't get comfortable to the point of laziness. Keep enjoying each other.*

38. *If your husband/boyfriend enjoyed what you did when you were dating, don't expect that to change.*

39. *Be honest with yourself and decide if you are going to be happy doing what you both do together for the duration of your relationship.*

40. *Be that girlfriend. Don't think because you are married, that you can let yourself go.*

41. *Be yourself, Love your man and try to understand him and the changes he goes through every day.*

42. *Don't let the world make you change, or make you think something is missing when it's all there.*

43. *Just enjoy life together.*

44. *Knowing that life can be over at any time, take advantage of the time you have with one another*

45. *Try not to complain.*

46. *Motivate your man.*

47. *Become a friend to your mate. Understand his hobbies and participate with him.*

48. *Don't be critical of his failures. If you make a man feel like a winner consistently, then in turn he will make the woman feel like a queen daily.*

49. *He needs your energy in order to give everyone in his household the very best that God desires for them.*

50. *Don't compete against your mate; be his partner, and in the end you will be blessed beyond measure. Why? Because you denied yourself at that time and in the end, the very thing you desired will be more than you imagined.*

51. *Keep doing the girlfriend things and keep as much of your size as you can.*

52. *Remember what attracted you to each other and do whatever is necessary to rekindle or revisit that.*

53. *From time to time, stop and ask what you need from each other. Decide if you are willing to change.*

54. *Always be able to change your mind to the love channel, like cable.*

55. *Keep looking so good that when you are out with your husband, he notices at least one or two other men doing a double take on you.*

56. *We husbands like to know that we still have a prize (although on a deep level we know that we have a good woman that no other can match). However, it means a lot to a man to have it confirmed by other brothers (it resonates with that hunter instinct that we've got "the one" that other men could not get or let get away).*

57. *Keep up the physical appearance.*

58. *More sex.*

59. *Know who your man truly is; know yourself and what you can live with and what you can't live without.*

60. *Trust God's process and admit your own faults. Each person has to stand before CHRIST, and will be responsible for his or her own actions.*

61. *Just because your husband is a poor leader does not relieve the wife of the responsibility of following him. On the converse, just because the wife is a poor follower does not mean the husband is void of his responsibility to lead.*

62. *Keep your appearance up — we do notice and we all want a good-looking wife!*

63. *Keep your sense of humor — there's nothing better than a great laugh!*

64. *Understand the basics of investing, financial planning and money management.*

65. *Great topic to bring life back into relationships. It is very critical. Do not take each other for granted. This topic needs to be discussed openly; the longer it stays silent, the worse things will become.*

66. *Be your husband's/boyfriend's FRIEND! If the two of you ARE friends, you'll be able to talk through the tough times. Also, talking is huge! If a guy WON'T talk to you BEFORE you get married, why*

would you expect him to talk after? For a marriage to survive there MUST be COMMUNICATION!

67. *Life is too short for a marriage to be bad.*

68. *The things that my friends and I have issues with are finances and appearance. Most men want eye-candy - they want to be with and be seen with a woman that takes care of herself (and him). If you looked fine when he was chasing you, he still wants that look twenty years later. If taking time off work to raise the kids is what you agree to do then find something else (like volunteering) to prevent you from just sitting around. No man wants an inactive woman.*

69. *Don't ask for more than you're willing to give.*

70. *If you expect total loyalty be willing to give the same.*

71. *Be honest. My ex-wife was not honest about being bisexual. That fact didn't bother me. The fact that she lied about it is what caused the damage. She became a mean person because she was trying to live a lie.*

72. *You have to live in the present with no regard to the future.*

73. *Life's changes cause us to lose touch with each other although we need more of each other. As lovers, we*

need to create our own world around the world we live in.

74. *Sit down and talk to each other. Listen to each other's issues. Most of all say what you mean, and mean what you say to each other.*

75. *Keep unqualified people out of your life.*

76. *If your friends have never been married or have multiple divorces, unless they can be transparent on why they have not been married or have so many divorces, then don't accept their advice on what you "should do."*

77. *Truly become one with your mate. Mama, Daddy, brother and sister should all take a backseat to your mate. For example, if little sister is bad with money and now she risks repossession, although she has kids a little pain and discomfort may be good for her. If you consistently bail out family or friends, you take away (tear apart) that proper cleaving to your mate. God has to place decisions in both of your hearts. Be honest; don't manipulate and/or hide things. If you do, then deep down your mate will say that he cannot trust you, or that you are not dependable.*

78. *Please, please, please pray together, study the Word together, fellowship together and minimize the auxiliary groups you belong to.*

79. *Every now and then, hang out with an elderly couple. There is a reason why they have been together 40, 50, or 60 years (they do exist). If you see them in a restaurant or church compliment them, and ask what made them stay together so long. God gives people wisdom to pass along to others.*

80. *Wives that make more money than their husbands should respect their husbands more if they are doing their best to provide for their families.*

81. *Life has many challenges; find time to just chat and recalibrate.*

82. *We want the girlfriend, and, in many ways, that can "affair proof" our marriages.*

83. *Just from observation, what makes an affair attractive on the front end is that it brings back all the infatuation and exhilaration that a husband misses in the girlfriend. Although the affair is destructive, short-lived passion, sinful, and ends in "death" of so many things we cherish, many men are willing to pay that price for the temporal*

adventure with the company of a "girlfriend" rather
than death by boredom.

The responses speak for themselves. We have heard
the complaint, many times, about husbands not having much to say about anything. Well, this time they
had much to say about how wives can recapture their
"girlfriend" sensibilities.

CHAPTER EIGHT

Would You Marry You?

"The first to apologize is the bravest. The first to forgive is the strongest. The first to forget is the happiest."
-Unknown

Now you have read the anonymous letters and survey results and recounted the interviews given by these husbands/ex-husbands. You can understand why I said that some of the input I received was hard to swallow, especially given what I know about how hard we as wives/ex-wives work/worked to be that perfect help mate, supporter and friend to our spouses. What do we do with ALL of this information? Should we ignore it and proclaim, like some of my fellow wives/ex-wives, that husbands/ex-husbands have issues too and should stop telling us what we need to do before they get themselves together? As hard as it is for me to say this after reading some of the results, I vote NO! I believe we take value from the fact that these husbands/ex-husbands took a risk in revealing their feelings (as some were too afraid to reveal their identities). We should seriously look at what we can do to make this a winning equation for us. Don't make this an easy sweep for the "Clean up Woman" as was proclaimed by songstress Betty Wright.

Vow to take back your power and work to become a girlfriend again; that Market Ready Sister/Market Ready Soul mate who is emotionally, financially, physically, professionally and spiritually where she wants to be or well on her way. How do we get there? I believe we first need to take an honest self-assessment. Ask yourself, this simple question, "Would you marry yourself in your current state?" If your answer is no, then take some time to self-reflect and figure out those prongs that are reflective of a Market Ready Sister/Market Ready Soul mate that you need to work on to bring you back to the market ready state you desire. None of us will likely have the same amount of work to do as your market ready state may not be my market ready state; so please don't fall into the mode of comparing, something that too many of us women do today which gets us nowhere. Stay focused on your market ready journey and encourage others along the way. Also, return to this book for encouragement or let this be a fuse to get you angry enough to go to that spa, do that sit up or work on your finances.

If you have old tapes playing in your head about things that your husband has done that you think you can't get past, then think about one response I was offered. A well-known actress, who is married to a very famous actor, said, when asked how she has managed to stay married for so long, "You have to have amnesia." Either you are going to forget some things and move on or you will stay stuck in your "angry depressed state" and go nowhere. Even doing nothing is doing something and that may lead to a dead end with the last rites being given to your relationship earlier than you desire. If, however, you have honestly done all that is possible and if your husband decides that he doesn't want to be with you, girlfriend or otherwise, then you make sure that you have lived your most conscious life in your role as wife, as purposefully invested in yourself as in the man you love. Stay fabulous and on top of your game, so that, if your marriage does, unfortunately, end, you will not simply be remembered by your husband, but missed. I'm absolutely convinced that, if you are market ready, you will definitely be missed although he will likely never admit it. Excuse me while I give you two snaps and a bag of veggie chips! (You know that I am watching my "girlfriend" figure, and, hopefully, you are watching yours.)

While, as I said earlier, this book is not intended to save marriages, or to be a panacea for any marital issue, I do hope that those who took the opportunity to read it will reflect on what they can do to strengthen their marital relationships. We know that marriage is not easy. Heck, relationships, in general, are not easy. But what good things have come from something easy? I like a challenge. Are you going to take on the challenge and get ready to declare that you are a real M.R.S...that Market Ready Sister/Market Ready Soul mate who is a wife and girlfriend too? I am cheering you on. So, get on your mark, get set, go!

ACKNOWLEDGMENTS

I have so much and so many people to be thankful for. First, I want to thank my Lord and Savior Jesus Christ for without you I am nothing.

To all of the anonymous husbands and ex-husbands who took a chance to reveal your feelings about wives as girlfriends, I appreciate you more than you know and it would have been impossible for me to deliver this message without you. I pray that your relationships benefit from these words.

Yogi Blackmon, you are a master of your craft. We bonded in Christ. You are a beautiful spirit and a talented writer/editor. I thank God for you.

Lidia Wylangowska, you are a fabulous artist! Our meeting was not a coincidence. Your art captures the heart and takes us on a beautiful journey. Thank you for sharing your gift with the world.

Bert Asbury, thank you for that "private" conversation we had in my closet. The surprise you exhibited when stumbling upon one of my "girlfriend" outfits still causes me to chuckle.

My sisters, Zonnie Bunch Smith and Lavern Bunch, thank you for your honest feedback. Your generous comments were greatly appreciated.

My niece, Frankie Bauldrick, I always thought you were smart, but now I have to also add wise. Thank you for your seasoned advice and gentle prodding. I appreciate you more than you know.

To my co-workers: Geneva Sturges, Alice Wang, Emily Charron, Tessa Gomes and Diane Vidmar, thanks for never growing weary of my wife as a girlfriend comments.

My friends, Dr. Erica and Mr. Russell Sails, thanks for living and loving in the open and inspiring me to move forward as God directs. You are special.

Ramona Haynes, Dr. Faye Barclay-Shell, Sherell Fuller, Rose Miller, Tracey Duval, Wynette Head, Dawn DuVerney Wilkins, Jacqueline Powell, Leslie Mundy, Mary Catchings, Linda Jackson, Donna Moss, Giovanna Hughes, Stacey Scales, Angelique David, Lauretta Hines, Evon Sheppard and Charisse Lillie, thanks for your encouragement and support as I forged ahead on this book's topic.

My daughter, Maya, thank you for giving me the space to write this book. You are a brilliant, humble and beautiful young lady who inspires me to be better.

Last, but certainly not least, my husband, Harry, thank you for giving me the reason to write this book. Your "uncut" and "unexpected" comments will now serve as an inspiration to "girlfriends" everywhere.